IMAGES
of England

KING'S HEATH

King's Heath House and Park in the winter, 1974.

IMAGES
of England

KING'S HEATH

Compiled by
Margaret D. Green

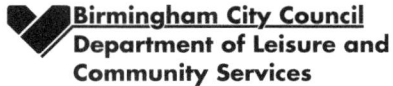

Birmingham City Council
Department of Leisure and
Community Services

TEMPUS

First published 1998
Copyright © Margaret D. Green, 1998

Tempus Publishing Limited
The Mill, Brimscombe Port,
Stroud, Gloucestershire, GL5 2QG

ISBN 0 7524 1555 7

Typesetting and origination by
Tempus Publishing Limited
Printed in Great Britain by
Midway Clark Printing, Wiltshire

Contents

Introduction 7

Acknowledgements 8

1. High Street, Side Roads 9

2. Old Farms and Houses 29

3. New Estates 45

4. The Road South 57

5. Churches and Schools 69

6. Stations, Bridges, Trams 83

7. Leisure 95

8. The South 117

9. Journey's End 125

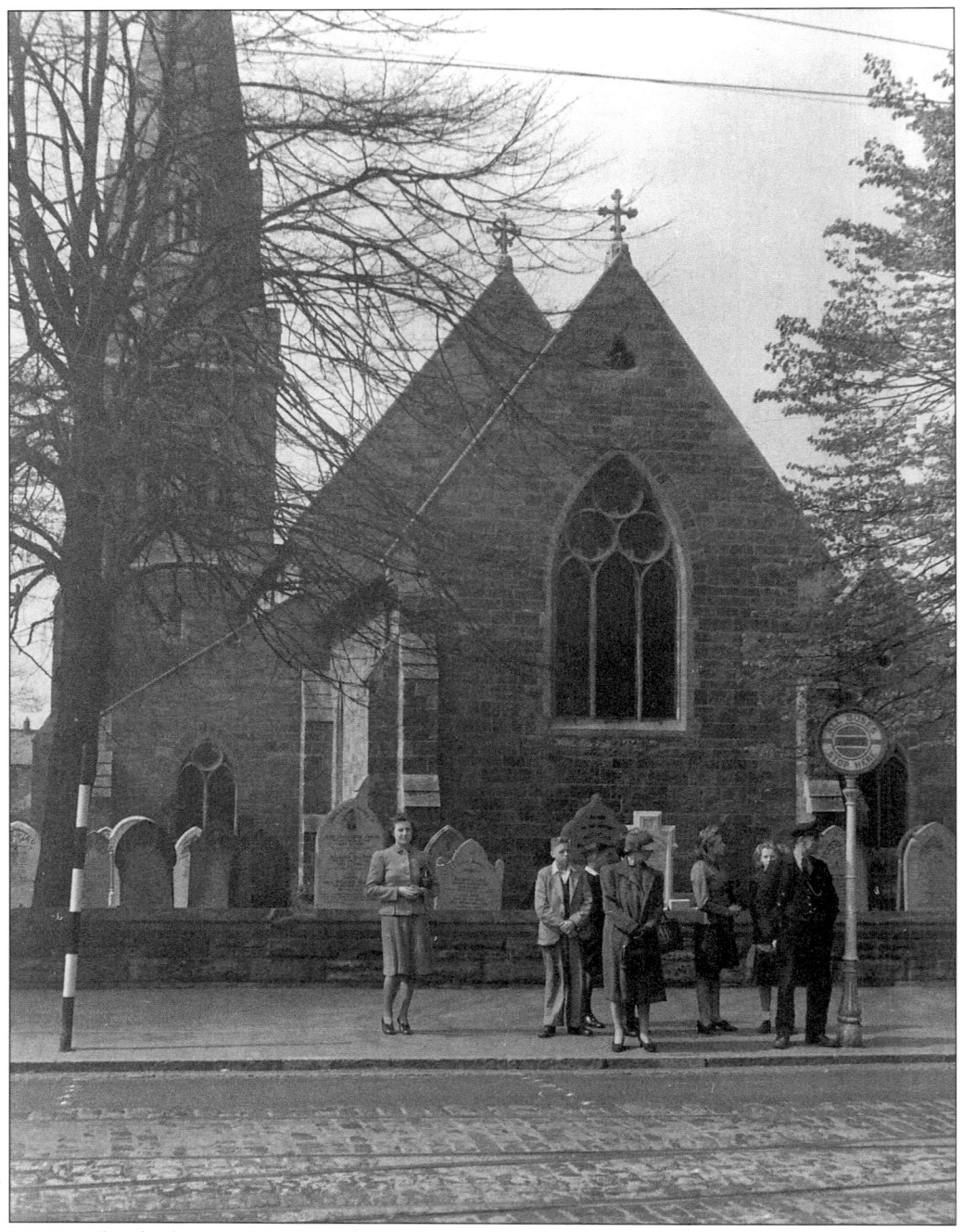

Waiting for the bus outside All Saints' church, *c.* 1945.

Introduction

The settlement and development of the King's Heath district essentially began during the eighteenth century. Until then, it was a largely unoccupied wasteland with ancient woods and commons. As part of the Royal Manor of King's Norton, this wasteland came to be called the King's Heath. The attractions of the area were timber, soil, suitable for brickmaking, and flax. In 1737, Pineapple Farm offered for sale twenty-nine oak, thirty ash and one beech tree, foretelling the loss of the ancient woods. In 1782, land was advertised as suitable for the residence of a genteel family, or for manufacturing, as coal was readily available from Birmingham. Two particular events attracted new settlers at this time. In 1767, the old track from Alcester to Birmingham was improved and became a turnpike road. The toll gate and house were probably located at the northern end of what is now the High Street, near the boundary with Moseley. This stretch of the road was then quite marshy, being much lower than the road to the south, but nevertheless a scattering of cottages appeared around the Cross Guns where travellers stopped for rest and refreshment. The second event was the further enclosure of the heath from 1772 when new farms were made in a circle around it.

Until 1800, the most important private house was Hazelwell Hall, built on an estate dating back to 1325. Now wealthy manufacturers from Birmingham began to buy farms and land here. William Hamper at the Grange and John Cartland at the Priory were both sons of Birmingham brassfounders. Attracted by its healthy air, the fine views to the south and its convenience to the town, such new settlers began the growth of King's Heath as a residential district. A railway station opened in 1840, providing quicker access to Birmingham. The largest business enterprise throughout the century was the brewery, founded in 1831. Ordinary people mostly worked on the farms or in small handicrafts. By 1840, there were many small businesses servicing the local community: grocers, bakers, beersellers, wheelwrights and blacksmiths, builders and bootmakers. The High Street was still called the Turnpike Road, and Vicarage Road was known as Black or Bleak Lane. Broad, Haunch, Billesley, Wheeler's and Dad's Lanes already existed. Silver Street was the last road in the village and consisted of a few houses and gardens.

After 1850, the district began to change dramatically. The population grew to an estimated 1,460 in 1865. It was 1,982 in 1871, 2,829 in 1881 and 4,610 in 1891. New churches, chapels and schools were built. The trams arrived in 1886, increasing access to Birmingham, but work could now also be found at Stirchley and Lifford. Large brickworks between Grove Road and King's Road supplied materials for new building in the area. By the 1880s, Valentine, Poplar and Woodfield Roads were filling up with large Victorian houses. In 1900, the police station had a staff of ten, with a local court for licensing and for rating appeals. The fire station, established in 1886, had eight men. There was also a flourishing social life, much of it taking place at the Institute, with cricket, tennis, football and bowling clubs, choral groups and the inevitable Temperance Society. The sale of the Grange estate in 1895 marked a change in house building locally. After decades of small, piecemeal and speculative building, the new Grange estate introduced the first planned housing estate in King's Heath.

At the turn of the century, King's Heath was still growing and prosperous. Trade, Ratepayers and Property Owners Associations existed, with many members hoping for independence from King's Norton. King's Heath and Moseley were by far the most important parts of King's Norton Urban District. Attempts by the Urban District Council to reduce street lighting in King's

Heath had been stopped and the lack of consultation concerning a new gas scheme was strongly criticized. Large individual houses were now spread south along the Alcester Road, among the old cottages. Featherstone, Tenbury and Livingstone Roads were laid out. Local pride was shown in the planting of 228 trees along the Alcester Road, 'for the welfare and betterment of the district' and paid for by public donations. In the same year, 1906, the local Committee for the Relief of the Poor reported an almost total absence of unemployment. Most of the residents were working class and, although employed, they did not however enjoy a good standard of living. Local wages were poor and did not compare with those in the workshops and factories in Birmingham.

Ambitions for independence were doomed and in 1911 Birmingham acquired King's Heath under the Greater Birmingham Scheme. Ironically, the growth of the district throughout the nineteenth century was due to its proximity to Birmingham, but it was this proximity which in the long term sealed its fate. Birmingham already supplied its gas and water and proceeded to develop King's Heath as a residential suburb for people from its overcrowded and unhealthy slums. Farms disappeared under private and municipal estates but the ancient open spaces at Billesley Common and Cocks Moor have been partly preserved.

Since 1945, the motorcar has brought mixed blessings: the traffic congestion is infamous, but the High Street needs cars and buses to survive as a retail centre. The Institute and Board School, and many Victorian shops, have been lost to modern retail needs. The High Street remains a centre of activity with the new community centre close by, as well as chain stores, small businesses, an indoor market in the old TASCOS Branch 24 and even a craftsman in stained glass works locally. A few minutes walk from the bustling High Street leads to the quiet, secluded roads of Victorian villas. In the west lies the splendid park with spacious roads of detached and semi-detached houses of the 1930s nearby. There is no medieval church or green here, but its origin as a nineteenth century village gives King's Heath character and distinction.

Acknowledgements

The majority of the photographs used here are from collections held by Birmingham Library Services. Thanks to Central Library, Local Studies and History Service for the use of the following pictures on the following pages: 2, 6, 9, 12b, 14, 16b, 20, 21a, 24-26, 27b, 30-40, 41b, 42b, 44-50, 51b, 52-57, 58b, 59-60, 66-68, 71, 72b, 75-76, 77b, 79a 81, 82b, 85a, 86-91, 92a, 93-98, 105-108, 109a, 110-128; Birmingham City Archives for: 28a, 61-65; King's Heath Community Library for: 10, 13, 17b, 18, 27a, 29, 42, 83-84; Judith Rosen of King's Heath Local History Society and Pauline Caswell of King's Heath Community Library who were both helpful when I first began looking for photographs. I am particularly grateful to Stan Budd for permission to use prints from his splendid collection of photographs of King's Heath past and present.

I thank the following for permission to use photographs which they have taken or collected. Stan Budd for: 10-11, 13, 15, 16a, 17-19, 22-23, 27a, 28b, 29, 31b, 38-39, 40b, 41a, 42a, 43, 51a, 58a, 67, 69-70, 72a, 73-74, 77b, 78, 80, 82a, 91, 92b, 113b, 123b, King's Heath Local History Society for: 11, 12a, 15, 16a, 17a, 19, 21b, 22-23, 28b, 41a, 43, 51a, 58a, 69-70, 73-74, 77a, 78, 79b, 80, 82a, 85b, 92b, Graham Proffitt and the Birmingham, King's Heath and Hall Green Photographic Society for: 21a, 40a, 47b, 90a, 105a, 108, 116b, 117-118, Peter Hunt and King's Heath Cricket and Sports Club Ltd for: 99-104, 109b, R.S. Carpenter for: 85b

Finally, I would like to thank Martin Flynn of Birmingham Library Services for the opportunity to work on this project, and for his practical support.

One
High Street, Side Roads

Old cottages in the High Street, *c.* 1890.

Matthew Court's drapery shop *c.* 1896. This was at No. 76, between the Cross Guns and the Baptist chapel. In the doorway are Matilda Court and her daughter Dorothy, born in 1893.

Taylor's high-class grocery shop, opposite the railway station, *c.* 1910.

Albert Osman's second hand furniture shop, opposite Grange Road, *c.* 1910.

The High Street with a glimpse of the Kingsway cinema, 1949. This opened as a cinema in 1925 and changed to become a bingo hall in 1980.

The Parade, c. 1950. Built about 1930, it was set back from the main road allowing for possible widening of the High Street, one of many proposals over the years for solving the congestion problem.

The High Street, *c.* 1910. Safeway supermarket now occupies this site. William Bluck was here from 1896 until the 1920s, having taken over the shop from Charles Elton who was also the sub-postmaster next door. The butcher's business was thought to have been established in 1770. Post office customers had to look out for the animal carcass hanging outside!

Looking north along the High Street, *c*. 1950.

The Cross Guns public house, *c*. 1950. It has recently been refurbished and renamed the Goose and Granite.

The old Cross Guns Inn, 1897. Dating from the eighteenth century, it took its name from an innkeeper who was also a gunsmith. It was also known locally as the Pear Tree, after the tree outside, which was said to have been planted in 1788. The inn was licensed in 1831, the same year in which King's Heath Brewery (behind the inn) was established. The Bate family then owned both the inn and the brewery. The Cross Guns was also a general meeting place for the village and from the 1840s served as the local police court. The new public house, erected in 1897, was much bigger and more modern and was thought to be more appropriate to the growing importance of King's Heath.

The old Hare and Hounds, *c.* 1895. The inn is the building with the bay windows.

The Hare and Hounds, *c.* 1950. The old building was auctioned in 1900, with plans already in hand for a much grander one with a corner tower.

The High Street near York Road, c. 1895. This building also appears in the photograph opposite. It is unclear whether it was a shop, a house or another way into the Hare and Hounds.

The High Street near Silver Street, c. 1915. Thomas Avery's hardware shop, on the near left with the buckets hanging up outside, was the last shop in the street before the old church school.

Looking south along the High Street, *c.* 1930. The High Street has been a busy retail centre for a long time and its crowded pavements are not a recent feature. This long run of Victorian buildings has now almost entirely disappeared. The board school (right), with its tower and spire, was recently replaced by Scots Corner. Only the building on the corner of Heathfield Road survives. It began life as a Lloyds Bank.

The High Street, 1987. This view of Nos 137 and 139, before demolition, shows their design in detail, with Jacobean style gabling, moulded brickwork and stone bay windows. Designed as a unified block of nine shops, as seen opposite, it was a very grand addition to any suburban high street. Foster's had occupied a site near this corner of Heathfield Road since the early 1900s and reappeared in the new development.

Cambridge Road viewed from the Wesleyan church, *c.* 1900.

The other end of Cambridge Road, *c.* 1950.

Poplar Road looking down to the High Street, 1974. This view is much the same today.

Poplar Road at the corner with Valentine Road, 1976. A nursery school and the new junior and infants' school stand here now.

Silver Street fire station, c. 1900.

A fire brigade horse, c. 1900.

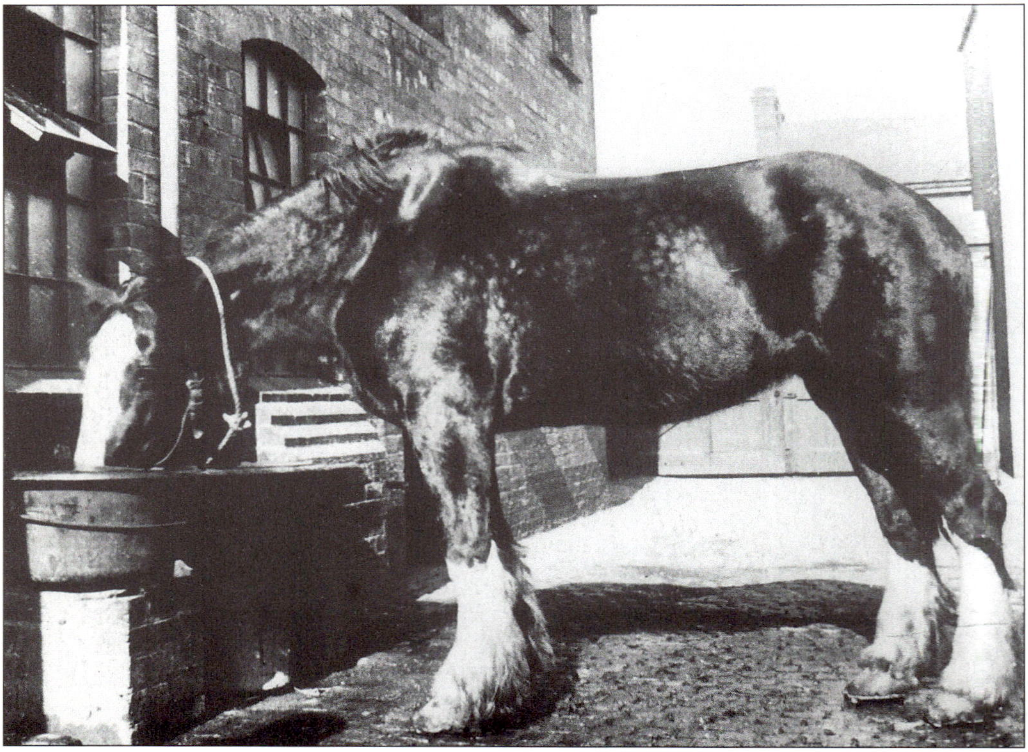

A fireman with horse-drawn pumps, c. 1900.

The exterior of the fire station, c. 1900. King's Heath Volunteer Fire Brigade was formed in 1886 and was the largest brigade in the King's Norton district.

Vicarage Road junction, with a horse trough and drinking fountain, *c.* 1890.

The same view, with a new shelter for the cabbies, *c.* 1900. The Birmingham tram, at the time, only reached Silver Street and anyone wishing to travel further south had to hire a cab or walk. Only the wealthy could afford their own carriages.

Vicarage Road junction, 1932. This corner is always changing! By now, public conveniences have been built underground and a new wrought-iron street lamp has replaced the old one. In 1994, the scene changed again when new conveniences replaced these, this time above ground. The outer circle bus service, which crosses the High Street at this busy corner, began in April 1926. It provided access from neighbouring suburbs bringing more people to the shops, the baths and activities at the Institute.

Vicarage Road, with neat, new houses, *c.* 1910.

Vicarage Road at the park, 1923. Colmore Road school is still just visible to the left.

Abbotts Road, *c.* 1900.

Vicarage Road near King's Road, by the tree, *c.* 1910.

The Old Red Lion at Grove Road, *c.* 1935. Built in 1904, the architects were J.J. Bateman and his son. Bateman Snr built many houses in King's Heath, which were described as comfortable but inexpensive. His son specialized in building large public houses.

Grove Road, with site of Colmore Road school on the left, *c.* 1900.

Two
Old Farms
and Houses

Haymaking at Dawberry Fields Farm, c. 1930.

The rear of Dawberry Fields Farm, one of the oldest in the district, *c.* 1930.

A farm cart at the Old Red Lion, *c.* 1930.

Brandwood House, 1900. Located at one of the highest points in King's Heath, it had excellent views. It was owned for over a century by the Gem family, who were well known attorneys and in 1890 G.F. Lyndon, the edge-tool maker, moved here. It is now part of a TAVR Centre.

Brandwood Farm, *c*. 1910.

Dad's Lane Farm, 1926. The farmhouse is on the left, with the barns in the centre. It was bought from J. Austen Chamberlain, in 1924, to be used for housing development.

A view of the old barns which were used as houses, 1926. The land around was being cleared for the new estate.

Joseph Henry Nettlefold (1827-81).

Kingsfield House, *c.* 1930. J.H. Nettlefold lived here until his death. Connected by marriage to the Chamberlains, the Nettlefolds were also their partners in the screw-making business until 1874. Joseph Henry donated money and land for the building of the Institute, as well as presenting twenty-six oil paintings by David Cox to the new Art Gallery in Birmingham. In 1924, Kingsfield House was acquired by the Roman Catholic church and was eventually demolished to make way for the new St Dunstan's church.

Hazelwell Hall, c. 1920. The house took its name from William de Haselwelle, who established an estate in the area from 1316, buying land, a mill, pastures and a moor. By marriage, it later became a seat of the Middlemores, former Lords of the Manor of Edgbaston. By 1840 it was merely a farm, but George Cartland moved here and modernized the old house. He was a founder of the Warwickshire County Cricket Club and played in the first match at the Edgbaston ground in 1886.

The Hazelwell public house, c. 1950. Built on the site of Hazelwell Hall when the Pineapple housing estate was being developed, the mock medieval design was clearly intended to reflect the historical importance of the site.

The Haunch, 1925. It was said to be the birthplace of Dr Johnson's mother, Sarah Ford, and in 1840 was owned by James Taylor, of nearby Moor Green. By 1916, it was being used as a convent and then as a mental hospital. It continued in institutional use, becoming a hostel in the 1960s. It was demolished around 1994 and the site was used for housing; only the large old trees nearby show that there was once a fine old house here.

The Priory, *c.* 1940. There had been a house on this site since the seventeenth century. In the early 1800s, it was the home of William Deakins, the sword and gun barrel maker of Sarehole Mill. It was then bought by James Cartland, the Birmingham brassfounder, for his son John. The house was altered and enlarged and was at first called Bleak House. John died in 1895 and his oldest son, John Howard Cartland, succeeded to the property. He was a senior partner in the firm but made plenty of time to travel the world and dabble in politics and sport. He died in 1940, unmarried, within weeks of two of his heirs going missing in France. The estate, the house and its contents were sold separately in August 1940.

John Howard Cartland in 1896, aged 46, in the uniform of a Captain of the Queen's Own Worcestershire Hussars.

The Priory, c. 1920. The grounds were often used for big social occasions. The early horse shows were held here as well as archery shoots, cricket matches and fêtes.

The small dining room, *c.* 1940. Cartland loved hunting and shot anything from edible deer to inedible exotic birds.

The conservatory, *c.* 1940. The zebra skin was no doubt 'bagged' on one of several trips to Africa. There was also a stuffed kangaroo in the house!

A sitting room, *c.* 1940. Family portraits, souvenirs of travels abroad and an odd mix of furniture styles are seen in this room.

A sitting room, *c.* 1940. A more elegant and stylish room, this was probably set aside for the ladies of the family.

The Priory Lodge, 1974. This was the gatehouse and is the only building remaining from the old estate. In 1956, the King Edward VI Grammar School Camp Hill, moved here and replaced the Priory with a new school.

Major Cartland's horse and trap, c. 1940. He loved horses and, although he owned a car, he still occasionally went into Birmingham in a horse-drawn vehicle.

King's Heath House, 1929. This was part of the Priory estate but was never lived in by the Cartlands. Frederick Everitt held annual picnics in the grounds for his employees at the brewery.

Belgian refugees at the house, 1914. In 1908, the house and grounds were bought to provide a much needed public park and the house was often used for such emergencies.

South Front.

Uffculme, *c*. 1900. Built by Richard Cadbury on the Henburys estate, it was named after the Cadburys' home village in Devon. It has been a centre for treating psychiatric disorders for many years. The wonderful solarium has recently been converted to office use.

The Henburys, 1931. When Cadbury built Uffculme on the hill above the original house on the Henburys estate, the old house was demolished except for this section. It was used as a refreshment room, known locally as the Bunkoms, when the grounds became a public park in 1922.

The Grange, with Isaac Bate and his family, *c.* 1890. This property was owned by the Hamper family until about 1869. William Hamper was a well known and respected antiquarian. While travelling for his father, a Birmingham brassfounder, he became interested in old churches, monuments and historic sites. He discovered that there were 140 different ways of spelling the name Birmingham! In 1895, after the death of Isaac Bate, the house and fifty-five acres of land were purchased by the Birmingham Freehold Society for redevelopment.

Hollybank Farm, with some of the new houses built around it on the right, *c.* 1950.

The Billesley Arms, 1925. An important old inn on the edge of the common, it was both a landmark and wilder than to is today. It was replaced in 1927 by the much grander public house which still stands and which was better suited to serve the growing local community.

Three
New Estates

Cutting Hollybank Road, *c.* 1938.

Chamberlain Road, c. 1950. The Hollybank estate flats were the first flats to be built in King's Heath, around 1930. The estate was founded in 1924 by Birmingham Mutual Housing and was a private scheme for a model village, aiming to preserve the rural delights of the site.

Hollybank Road, c. 1955. Financial problems and the war delayed the plans and, in 1954, the undeveloped land was bought for municipal housing.

The doctor's surgery, Chamberlain Road, *c.* 1950. Built about 1935, this stylish house shows the high aims of the estate.

Haunch Lane shops, one of the original features of the estate, 1974.

The junction of Haunch Lane and Wheeler's Lane, 1925. On the left is the site of Howard Road East.

The same junction but looking down Haunch Lane from Howard Road East, 1932.

Haunch Lane at Yardley Wood Road, before development, 1925.

The same view, with new municipal housing and the Tudor cinema, 1935.

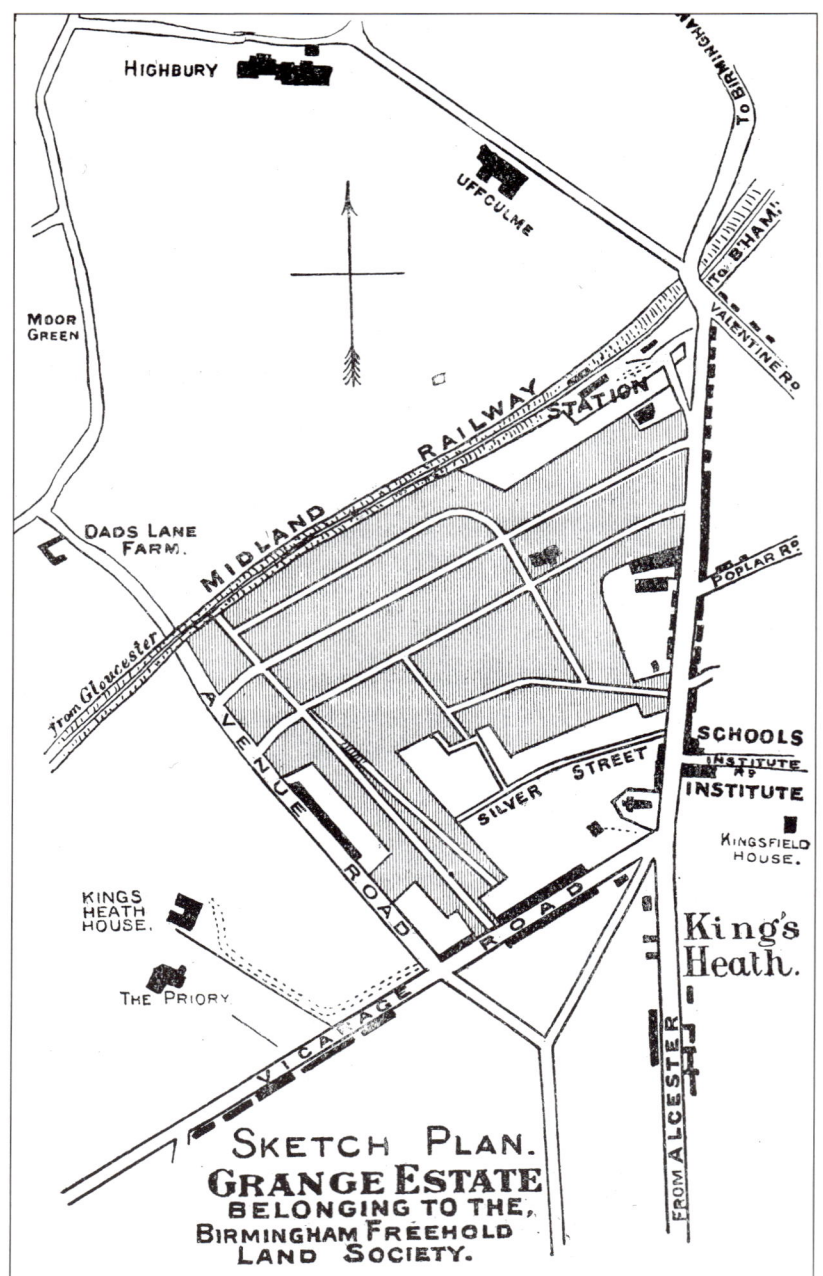

The Grange Estate, 1895. This was the fifty-sixth estate bought by the Birmingham Freehold Society for housing development. The old house was demolished but the new estate took on its name. The land was flattened and two miles of new roads were laid. The aim was to build 900 houses, with shops on the main road. The best houses would be close to the station and the cheapest next to the main road, but no back-to-back houses, terraces or public houses were allowed. The estate was not intended to make money for speculative builders, but to give an opportunity to artisans, clerks, teachers and the like to live in healthy suburban houses. It proved to be a popular concept and over 2,400 applications were received for 449 plots.

Station Road, *c.* 1910. The variety of styles is clear, a contrast to the uniform housing in many other roads in King's Heath of the same period.

A detail of the large, double-fronted houses, *c.* 1950.

Dad's Lane looking towards Avenue Road, with houses finished but not yet occupied, 1925.

Dad's Lane looking towards Moor Green, 1927. The old farm is in the distance. The hilly aspect of the land and many of the wooded dells were kept to preserve a rural aspect on this estate.

The Pineapple estate under construction, c. 1920. The land was bought, in 1913, for the first proposed municipal housing estate in Birmingham, but the war intervened. The estate is viewed from the railway embankment and in the distance can be seen piles of locally made bricks, ready for use.

The same view, showing the junction of Allen's Croft Road, Dawberry Road and Waldrons Moor, 1925. Brandwood House and the farm are just visible on the hill to the right. The chimney stacks belonged to the three brick works around King's Road.

Pineapple bridge, 1924. Many old roads and bridges in King's Heath were improved in the 1920s and '30s, because of the extra traffic brought by the new estates.

The same view in 1930.

Pineapple bridge looking to Vicarage Road, with the farm on the hill, 1924.

The same view, with new shops, 1930. The church of St Mary Magdalen, Hazelwell (left) began as a mission from All Saints' in 1906.

Billesley House estate, 1924. These houses in Menin Road and Jutland Road were standard municipal designs and can be seen throughout the city.

Menin Road houses, 1924, described as the Birmingham standard non-parlour type!

Four

The Road South

A view of Drayton Road, c. 1950.

Cranage's bakery shop, on the corner of Drayton Road, *c.* 1910.

Heathfield Cottage, *c.* 1900. Situated between Middleton Road and Albert Road, with its pretty topiary garden, it was more than just a cottage. The rear portion was a two-storey, double-gabled block, twice the size of the front cottage, with a side conservatory and large outhouses. It was the home of Joseph Moss Todd who was, for many years, the publican of the King's Arms.

Looking north at Howard Road, 1926. This mixture of houses represents over a century of development along the Alcester Road South. On the right, the nearest houses are early nineteenth-century cottages, with a late Victorian, three-storey villa in the distance. On the left side of the road are new semi-detached areas of central Birmingham.

Cutting Howard Road East, 1931. A children's park is now on the site of this house, also shown in the above photograph, on the right.

A drinking fountain and horse trough, Alcester Road South, *c.* 1950. It was located at the junction of Featherstone and Tenbury Roads and commemorated Queen Victoria's Diamond Jubilee in 1897. This kind of public facility was common in the nineteenth and early twentieth centuries, but have now largely disappeared from our streets.

A formal studio portrait of Fred and Agnes Mary Cottrell, with four of their children, c. 1895. Agnes came here from Chester with her parents and sisters in 1882 and settled in Douglass Villas, Alcester Road, opposite the present Masonic Hall. Her father, Thomas Noyes, was a bookmaker. Fred's father was a builder who moved to Birmingham in the 1850s, from the same village as the Cadburys, Uffculme in Devon. Like other middle class families, Charles Cottrell was attracted by the rural aspect of King's Heath and in 1880 moved into Featherstone Road.

Agnes Mary Burgess Noyes before her marriage to Fred Cottrell, aged 20, c. 1884.

Agnes and Fred Cottrell's children, Dorothy, Fred and Bertie, c. 1892.

Agnes Cottrell in the garden, aged around 40.

The Cottrells and their six children, with Aunt Amy Noyes, on a country drive, c. 1898. The building trade was booming so Fred could well afford his own carriage. A family tradition tells that they built Walford Road Ice Rink but were never paid for it. The client called on a Sunday to pay, but Fred would not do business on the Sabbath!

A young Walter Tomlinson, the proud owner of a penny-farthing bicycle, *c.* 1885.

The wedding party of Walter Tomlinson and Kate Noyes, 1897. Walter's family had been in King's Heath since the 1860s and his father made fenders and fire-irons.

A tennis party at Livingstone Road, *c.* 1910. The Tomlinsons moved here to a house called Eastnor in 1906. Kate was a teacher and lived to the age of 99.

Brooklands Tennis Club was conveniently at the end of the Tomlinsons' back garden.

Alcester House, 1909. Built about 1860, it was then a country retreat for the succession of Birmingham manufacturers who lived here. Too large to remain a private house, it has survived as the Loyal Calendonian Corks Social Club.

These extensive grounds, with ornamental walks, orchards and an orangery, became the site for the Masonic Hall.

Alcester Lane's End at Woodthorpe Road, *c.* 1910. In 1907, when the tram service was electrified, the line was extended to the King's Arms.

The same view, with houses converted to shops, *c.* 1920. The tram and the dog track brought business to this part of the road.

Looking south to Millpool Hill, 1935. The cottages were in Broad Lane. The stream in the valley is the Chinn Brook, running east to Yardley Wood and the River Cole. The houses on the horizon faced Millpool Hill Farm, where the Alcester Road turns east. This area was a local beauty spot, best appreciated on foot.

Five
Churches and Schools

Christadelphians, Institute Road, c. 1910.

The choir, Wesleyan Methodist church, Cambridge Road, *c.* 1950.

The interior before the pews were removed, *c.* 1950.

Wesleyan Methodist church, *c.* 1910. The first place of worship in King's Heath was a cottage in Avenue Road, around 1870. Later, a chapel school was built in School Road and, when larger premises were needed, this church was built on the corner of Cambridge Road. Opened in 1896, it is a splendid Gothic, red brick and terracotta design, with a spire and stained glass windows, decoration not usually associated with Methodists.

Colmore Road school, 1990. Begun in 1909, it was meant to ease overcrowding at the Board School. The first classes were taught in King's Heath House, causing Major Cartland to complain about the noise!

The war hospital, 1915. Because it was close to a station, this school was chosen to be an annex of the 1st Southern General War Hospital, at the university. The children were transferred to Institute Road.

Colmore Road school, girls' dramatics class, 1932.

Excellent costumes for the story of Moses.

Girls at Colmore Road School, *c.* 1925.

Unidentified dramatics, 1931.

All Saints' church, 1875. Before the church school was licensed for services, worshippers travelled to Moseley or further afield which was difficult without transport and in bad weather. All Saints' was consecrated as a chapel of ease for Moseley in 1860, before King's Heath became a parish in its own right. Construction was plagued by money problems and the spire was added in 1866 at the expense of the Misses Anderton of Wake Green. The original roof tiles were laid in the diaper pattern seen here. The school building, on the right, continued in use as a church hall.

The exterior of the church, with gravestones upright, *c.* 1940.

The exterior of the church, with the gravestones laid flat for easy maintenance, 1954. Interested parties had to be consulted first, but only 7 out of 130 objected and theirs are the gravestones still standing. The buildings at the back were in Silver Street.

John Webster, his wife, family and curates in the vicarage garden, *c.* 1880. He was vicar here for twenty years before he died in 1886.

The church's interior, *c.* 1940. The wrought-iron chancel screen was donated by the Cartland family, in 1893, in memory of Mr and Mrs John Cartland.

A mixed group of urchins at the Board School, *c.* 1890.

A boys' class, *c.* 1890. The school was built on the High Street in 1878. It was originally planned to accommodate 220 infants, as well as 150 boys and 150 girls, but was extended down Institute Road as the local population increased.

A view of the school, c. 1890. The spire on the ventilation tower was pure decoration, meant to show that the school was important in the community and of equal status with the church.

Proud winners of the Junior Football Shield, 1937/38.

An infants' parents day, 1927.

An infants' class, 1922.

The Baptist church, the High Street, *c.* 1910. Non-conformists were recorded in King's Heath as early as 1791, in connection with the Priestley Riots. In the riots, the house occupied by John Harwood, a blind Baptist, was destroyed followed by the house of Mr Cox in Warstock. In 1811, the Baptist community was using a small cottage for worship, before erecting a meeting house and school on part of the site occupied by the present church. This building was opened in 1898 and was intended to have had a spire when funds permitted.

The interior of St Dunstan's Roman Catholic church, *c.* 1930. The first St Dunstan's was a corrugated iron building in Station Road which was destroyed during an air raid in 1940.

The interior of St Dunstan's, 1956. The congregation had now moved to Kingsfield House which became the site of the new St Dunstan's.

Six

Stations,
Bridges, Trams

King's Heath railway station staff, *c.* 1920.

Dixon and Baker, coal merchants at the station, *c.* 1910. Coal was delivered twice daily to the station and was sold on by the eight merchants based there in 1910.

Station staff at the signal box, *c.* 1920.

King's Heath station, *c.* 1905. The station was opened in 1840, on the Birmingham to Gloucester line and, until 1867, was called Moseley Station. In 1906, there were eight passenger trains to Birmingham before nine o'clock in the morning.

The closed station, 1966. As a war economy, passenger traffic ceased in 1941 and only goods were carried. The line is now a through route for freight and the station buildings have been demolished.

Dad's Lane railway bridge, 1931.

The same view after improvements, 1932.

Working on the bridge, 1931.

Workmen and locals pose for the camera – regardless of the hazards!

Reconstruction of Cartland Road bridge, 1928. Hazelwell station, visible in the distance was opened in 1906 at the request of residents of the Brandwood End area which was then being developed.

The bridge from above, with a view of the rather grand ticket office. Hazelwell station closed in 1941.

A steam tram in Silver Street depot, 1889. The steam tram route was extended to King's Heath in 1887, taking over from the slow and infrequent horse bus. It was seen as a crude transport development, ugly, smelly, noisy, cumbersome and dangerous. It was also convenient, cheap, democratic and not cruel to horses!

An electric tram at the King's Arms, 1935.

Trams at Alcester Lane's End, *c.* 1930. They ran here to and from Hill Street until 1949, when they were replaced on this route by motor buses.

A delightful studio portrait of a young tram conductress, *c.* 1916. Many women were able to work outside their homes for the first time during the First World War which then freed men for military service or war work.

The Tramways Department war memorial, *c.* 1990. It was erected at the Wheeler's Lane Stadium in 1922, in memory of the 326 employees who died during the First World War.

A motor bus on the cross city service from King's Heath to Bearwood, *c.* 1922. The unfortunate driver had no protection from bad weather.

Canal bridge at Millpool Hill, 1938. The Stratford Canal, completed in 1816, crosses the Alcester Road South at this point and joins the Birmingham to Worcester Canal at King's Norton locks.

The same view, looking west to King's Norton, with the road and bridge much improved, 1939.

The east portal, Brandwood Canal tunnel, 1926. Although only the carved head now survives, this tunnel entrance is a listed building. The canal provided a vital transport connection between Birmingham and mid-Warwickshire, particularly for carrying coal.

Seven

Leisure

King's Heath Park, 1915.

King's Heath House, an elegant house in a beautiful setting, *c.* 1960. Since 1908, it has had many uses: a temporary school, a home for refugees, a war hospital and a hostel for discharged soldiers training in agriculture. The School of Horticulture began here in 1952, when the Parks Department introduced a training scheme for its staff. The park's long association with television started in 1972 with Bob and Cyril's weekly advice show. Pershore Horticultural College has a base here and each September the city holds a popular gardeners' weekend in the park.

The plot belonging to BBC *Children's Hour* radio programme, tended by local schoolgirls, c. 1955.

A classroom in the School of Horticulture, 1954. Training for the Parks Department apprentices was essentially practical, ranging from maintenance of golf courses to growing grapevines. Classroom teaching was restricted to the basics of botany.

The obelisk in Highbury Park, 1957. It marked the burial place of a favourite racehorse of the Lyndons who lived at on the Henburys estate in the nineteenth century.

The Italian Garden in Highbury Park, 1955. In 1922, the Civic Society bought forty-two acres of the Henburys estate to add to Uffculme and Highbury Parks alongside the railway line.

King's Heath Cricket Club, Vicarage Road, *c*. 1890. Founded in 1868, it is the oldest existing sports club in King's Heath. George Cartland was an early player and was president at the turn of the century. Sir John Holder and Austen Chamberlain served as vice presidents and many players have represented Warwickshire County. It did not have a permanent home until 1927, when the present clubhouse and grounds at No. 247 Alcester Road South were purchased. The club's other sports include archery, bowls, hockey, tennis and squash, with snooker in the clubhouse.

Tennis at the Barn Lane grounds, *c.* 1914. The club also had allotments here.

Miss Perkins at the wicket, *c.* 1914.

Bowling at Barn Lane, c. 1914.

The bowls section, 1932.

A river outing, *c.* 1914.

A club social at the Masonic Hall, 1927.

King's Heath Cricket Club 1st XI, 1925.

King's Heath Cricket Club 1st XI, with the old pavilion in the background, 1933.

Children watching Punch and Judy, on ladies' day, *c.* 1960. The rear of the house has since been extended and squash courts erected in the garden.

The ladies' day raffle in the billiards room, *c.* 1960. Women were not allowed to be members in their own right at that time, but families were made welcome at regular ladies' days with hospitality and entertainment organized by the men.

Cocks Moor golf course, with the last remnants of the ancient woodland of King's Heath, 1974.

The thatched clubhouse, 1930. Opened in 1926, Cocks Moor was the fourth municipal golf course in Birmingham.

A water gala celebrating the opening of King's Heath public baths, 1923. The baths closed in 1987.

Councillor Goodby, chairman of the Baths Committee, presiding over the opening ceremony. Goodby lived at Brandwood End and was a keen supporter of local sports.

The pool could was over for indoor sports or dancing, c. 1930.

The attendants office, 1923. Beyond this point were forty private baths for washing, provided because many homes still lacked proper bathrooms.

An exterior view of the baths, showing the rear of the Institute, 1974.

A High Street view of the Institute, 1974. Woolworths first leased the site in 1933, building a store in place of the main hall and basement.

The Institute in 1907. As well as J.H. Nettlefold, the Cartlands and Isaac Bate also contributed towards the cost of the building. Begun in 1878, it had a library, lecture hall and newsrooms and was for many years the centre of social life for working class residents of King's Heath.

King's Heath Albion, 1913/14, a football team started at the Institute in 1890.

The Working Mens' Club, 1904. It had met in the Institute basement since 1882, but was forced out by the Woolworths takeover in 1933; it only survived for two more years. These are working men in their Sunday Best!

King's Heath Horse Show committee and council, 1921. The show began in 1899 as a May Day parade of working horses used by the railway, brewery and local tradesmen. Seated in the centre, with his dog, is Major Cartland.

Watching the show, *c.* 1955. The first shows were held at Highbury Hall and the Priory, before moving to the Alcester Lane's End ground in 1923. They continued annually on Whit Monday until about 1965.

An advert for greyhound racing, 1928. The show ground was converted for greyhound racing in 1926.

THE BRITISH GREYHOUND
:: SPORTS CLUB LIMITED ::

GREYHOUND

RACES

ALCESTER LANES END

Mondays, Wednesdays & Saturdays

Commencing at 7-30 p.m.

CLEAN, EXHILARATING
HUMANE SPORT

An aerial view of the dog track, c. 1930. There were other entertainments at the ground, such as rugby in winter and once a riding display by Russian Cossacks. Ann Haydon Jones, the Wimbledon Champion, learned to play tennis here.

The exterior of the public library, 1931. Built in 1906, it was paid for by Andrew Carnegie, the Scots/American philanthropist who made his fortune from steel. The building at the rear is the only part of the nineteenth-century police station which remains today.

The reading room, 1913. No conversation was allowed and a table was reserved for ladies!

The issue counter, 1913.

Another view of the reading room, 1913.

Tudor cinema, Haunch Lane, 1950. This glorious suburban cinema (built in 1929) was recently demolished and replaced by housing.

Football on Billesley Common, 1974. An important public open space, it is now only a remnant of the ancient common which stretched across the old turnpike road. Sometimes called King's Heath Common, it was the site of anti-aircraft defences in both wars.

116

Eight

The South

A picturesque view of the canal and old bridge at Millpool Hill, 1935.

Cottages at Millpool Hill, south of the canal, 1935.

Waterman's cottage on the canal, 1974.

Looking north at the Horse Shoe Inn, 1938.

The same view, with the road widened and the old cottages, on the left of the photograph above, cleared away, 1939.

Near the site of Glenavon Road, with Millpool Hill Farm on the left, 1934.

Limekiln Lane, *c.* 1930. It was probably laid when the canal was cut. Lime was needed to make mortar for tunnels and bridges and was burned on site from limestone brought in by the Stratford Canal Company.

The weigh house on the corner of Limekiln Lane, *c.* 1930. It was probably used to weigh large deliveries of coal arriving at the wharf by barge from Birmingham, before they were distributed further south by cart and later by lorry. The vehicle halted on a large metal plate in the road and its weight registered in the house. It was in use before 1900.

Laying a new road to Warstock, 1938.

The new municipal houses at Glenavon Road, 1947. The Millpool Hill estate was one of many post-war developments in the city which tried to solve the problems of slum housing and the shortage of housing worsened by the war.

A grove off Glenavon Road, 1947.

At the Maypole, looking north up the Alcester Road South, 1934.

The same view, with the supposed maypole, *c.* 1905. It originated as a signpost at this important junction on the turnpike road from Alcester. In the nineteenth century, May Day festivities were temporarily revived here, popularizing the use of 'Maypole' as a local place name.

A store on the south bound corner of the Alcester Road South, 1934.

A view west down Druids Lane, with Maypole Farm on the right, 1937. Until the late nineteenth century, it was always known at Malthouse Farm.

Nine

Journey's End

The Woodthorpe Road entrance of Brandwood End Cemetery, 1933.

The registrar's house and office, *c.* 1920. The cemetery opened in 1899 and the first burial was that of a small child, a sign of harder times.

A general view of the chapel, with the early twentieth-century monuments in the foreground, *c.* 1920. The chapel was built on the highest point in the cemetery and dominates views along the main avenue.

The chapel, 1933. Now a listed building, it actually consists of two chapels, one Church of England and one Non-conformist. It is a splendid Gothic design, in red brick and terracotta, designed by Brewin Holmes, a local architect from Moseley. Its wide avenues, landscaped grounds and rural setting made Brandwood End instantly popular. The chapel foundation stone contained a time capsule with a print of the design, a seal of King's Norton District Council and a copy of the *Birmingham Weekly News*!

A peaceful view south through the archway of the chapel at Brandwood End Cemetery, 1933. Late Victorian cemeteries are increasingly appreciated not only as examples of landscape design and the stonemason's skill, but also as havens for wildlife in the urban environment. Here, the evergreen avenues of Scots pine, Wellingtonia and cypress are enriched from spring to autumn by deciduous trees such as beech and horse chestnut.